MACROBERT'S

MACROBERT'S REPLY

A STORY OF BRITISH RESILIENCE IN HISTORY'S DARKEST HOUR

Text Philip Hamlyn Williams, on behalf of Story Terrace,

with Philip Jeffs

Copyright © Philip Jeffs

Design Adeline Media, London

Printed and bound in Great Britain by Clays Ltd, St Ives plc

First print December 2016

www.StoryTerrace.com

TABLE OF CONTENTS

PREFACE

The story of the MacRobert's Reply is remarkable in many ways. It speaks of generosity, of bravery, of endurance – but for me, most of all, of loss. In writing this account, I am indebted first of all to Philip Jeffs who carried out much painstaking research for the website he created to get the story better known.

My own research has taken me deeper into the MacRobert family story and I am indebted to Marion Miller for her remarkable work, *From Cawnpore to Cromar: The MacRoberts of Douneside*. I have looked deeper into XV Squadron and am indebted to Martyn Ford-Jones for the books he wrote, in particular *Bomber Squadron: The men who flew with XV*, and the archive he maintains. I have explored the story of the Stirling bomber and Jonathan Falconer's book *Stirling Wings*. Anyone exploring Bomber Command during the Second World War would be the poorer had they not read *Bomber Boys: Fighting back 1940-45* by Patrick Bishop or *Bomber Command* by Max Hastings.

The administrative staff of XV squadron maintained detailed records of operations and the National Archives have digitised these and made them available. I am grateful to both but also specifically to the National Archive for the records of Lady MacRobert's correspondence with the Air Ministry from which I have drawn extensively. Finally, I say thank you to the Imperial War Museum for making recordings of the recollections of veterans and to the veterans themselves for telling their stories.

Philip Hamlyn Williams
Lincoln
11 December 2015

ACKNOWLEDGEMENTS

As the son of Don Jeffs, I in turn would like to express my gratitude to those who supported my efforts to create this book.

Denmark: Sq. Ldr Eric Jensen (Retired), Bent Henriksen, Erik Hansen, Finn Buch, Stig Johansen, Bo and Aksel Sommerby, and Lisbeth Behrendt. Thanks also to Jørgen Bertelsen for kindly allowing me access to his archive file, and thanks to Willy Schmidt for coming forward after 60 years as one of the men who helped my father escape from the crash site alive.

UK: Joe Sharp, Giuseppe Lombardi of the Stirling Project, Dennis Royston of the Stirling Aircraft Association, Gordon Leith of RAF Hendon Museum and Torben Harris (XV Sqn Association). Special thanks for his research and support to Roger Leivers of the 'Godmanchester Stirling', a sister aircraft to MacRobert's Reply also with XV Squadron.

New Zealand: Errol Martyn, John Ryan (see below).

Tasmania: Beryl Tasharofi.

To relatives of the crew: My thanks to the sister and niece of Sgt Ronald Maycock for supplying me with details of his RAF career. Thanks to the family of Sqn Ldr John Hall for verifying certain information regarding his RAF career before he took command of MacRobert's Reply W7531. Thanks to John Ryan, son of F/O John (Buck) Ryan (the Reply navigator) who provided much needed material all the way from New Zealand. Thank you also to the nephew of Sgt Bob Nicholson (rear gunner) who made contact in 2004 and has provided many useful items for the site.

Special thanks: Lastly, but most importantly, I wish to acknowledge an incredible man without who this book would not have any relevance to me, my father Donald Jeffs. My father flew in all of the MacRobert's Reply bombers and, as you will learn, his own story is incredible and has been interwoven into the history that you will read in this book. As a young boy listening to my father tell the story of the MacRobert's Reply, it became part of my childhood memories, and so I suppose I was destined at some point to collaborate on a book such as this. I dedicate this book to my father, Donald Jeffs.

Philip Jeffs

This book remembers with gratitude the crew of MacRobert's Reply W7531 Short Stirling of XV Squadron, who paid the ultimate sacrifice on the morning of 18 May 1942:

Sqn Ldr. John Charles Hall - Pilot 41693 RAF

Flt Lt. Neville George Richardson Booth – Pilot 81661 RAF

Flt Officer John Patrick (Buck) Ryan -
Navigator J4758 RCAF

Sgt. John Bernard Butterworth - Air Gunner 1307679 RAF

Sgt. Robert (Nick) Nicholson - Air Gunner 954208 RAF

Sgt. Frank (Frankie) Leslie Sharp - Air Gunner 91003 RAF

Sgt. Anthony (Spriggy) Spriggs - Flt. Engineer 568054 RAF

Sgt. Ronald (Ronnie) Maycock - Observer 1384147 RAF

FOREWORD
BY PAUL FROOME

I am honoured to have been asked, as the current Officer Commanding XV Squadron, to write the foreword to this book that describes life on a wartime bomber squadron and an event that is deeply ingrained in the Squadron's memory, even to this day. This is the tragic story of a mother whose three sons were killed in flying accidents – two early in the Second World War, the bravery of the aircrew of XV Squadron, and how the two came to be linked together for eternity.

In 1941 Lady MacRobert donated £25,000 to the Air Ministry to purchase a bomber aircraft, after her last surviving son, Sir Iain aged just 24, was lost on operations. The aircraft, a Shorts Stirling, was delivered to XV Squadron in October 1941 and at Lady MacRobert's request was named MacRobert's Reply. The aircraft flew with the family coat of arms emblazoned below the cockpit and the crew were incredibly proud to fly the aircraft and "...strike hard, sharp and straight to the mark," as Lady MacRobert described in a letter to the crew. Sadly, on 18 May 1942, the aircraft was shot down and eight of the nine crew on board lost their lives.

Every Royal Air Force squadron holds their history dear, and none more so than those who currently serve, and who have served, on XV Squadron. Flying Officer Peter Boggis DFC was the first captain of MacRobert's Reply and his logbook is a centrepiece on the Squadron, and in it is preserved the letter to the crew I mentioned earlier. Each year, at the invitation of the local 4th May Committee, marking the day the Message of Freedom was broadcast across Denmark, we parade our Squadron Standard at the crash site of MacRobert's Reply near Middelfart. Here we remember the sacrifice of the eight men who perished in the crash on 18 May and the courage of Donald Jeffs who so nobly endured the ardours of imprisonment. I have been privileged to attend this event, and the respect and feelings for the entire crew are as strong now as they were in the Second World War.

In 1982, XV Squadron rekindled the link with MacRobert's Reply and since that day an aircraft has flown on XV Squadron with the MacRobert Family crest, the name MacRobert's Reply, and the tail code 'F' just as the very first Stirling did. It has, by tradition, been the Bosses aircraft and I am incredibly proud to have my name painted on the canopy of the current MacRobert's Reply. The tradition to have 'F' flying is a mark of our respect for the MacRobert's family, our predecessors who fought for the freedom we enjoy today, and it keeps our Squadron history very much alive. The aircrew and groundcrew alike hold deep respect for the aircraft and reflect Lady MacRobert's wishes "…my thanks to those who have the care of my 'Reply', and prepare her for her flights.

The MacRobert family were generous benefactors to the Royal Air Force, and continue to be so through the MacRobert Trust and award prizes annually at the Royal Air Force College Cranwell and to the Air Training Corps. We maintain close links with the Trust and the Squadron's veterans who still visit the Squadron, and the first question they all ask is about MacRobert's Reply and whether she is still flying. I am always proud to show them 'F' and to tell them of the story you are about to read.

Wing Commander Paul Froome
Officer Commanding XV(R) Squadron, Royal Air Force
Lossiemouth, Moray
IV31 6SD 01343

INTRODUCTION

The evening of May 17th 1942 was clear and cloudless, but with no moon to speak of. That was why it had been chosen; less chance of being seen.

As the four massive Bristol Hercules engines started up, each producing nearly 1600 horsepower, the vibrations ran the length of the Short Stirling W7531 (call sign LS-F for Freddie), and through the men inside it. 'Men' was an easy term to use given the times they were in and the experiences they had endured as this plane's crew were mostly just above boys at best, including the skipper who was a veritable twenty-four. In fact, they were old by the standards of warfare at the time, where so many proud young sons had perished long before reaching their mid-twenties.

Squadron Leader John Hall D.F.C came over the intercom, *'crew get ready for take-off'*. There were smiles all round from the rest of the crew. Even at their tender ages they were already veterans of many flights and had been 'ready' from well before the engines were fired up, but the skipper liked to be thorough, which was why he was so well liked and admired by the men who flew with him. This was a close and friendly crew, well used to living in close company both on and off the big bomber. All the crew had already checked and re-checked their instruments and guns, knowing they would need the former to get where they were going, and in all probability the latter to be able to get home again.

The skipper and his co-pilot ran over the final instrument checks, received their final clearance from the tower, and commenced the long taxi run down to the main runway. They checked their watches and, looking at each other, gave a thumbs-up; timing was right on the button. As they reached the end of the taxi path and swung onto the runway the field ahead seemed enormous, but they knew they would need every inch of it to get this great beast into the sky.

Squadron Leader Hall looked across to his co-pilot and simply nodded; Neville Booth nodded back. No words were needed. Although they had never flown together before, they both knew the procedure. The co-pilot was not a regular member of this crew; he was an RAF observer for this flight only observing the new GEEE guidance system that was recently installed. They throttled the engines to full and with a mighty roar the big four-engined bomber started its long and painstakingly slow haul up the runway at RAF Wyton, fifty miles north of London. The huge aircraft gained speed at an impossibly slow rate, and inside everything was vibrating and shrieking in protest at the impossible demands being placed on the airframe. As the end of the runway came into view the pilot pulled back on his stick. The huge beast lifted its nose and rose slowly skywards. The fully laden take-off weight of some 32 tons required maximum thrust from the engines, and plumes of black smoke bellowed from the exhausts as the famously named MacRobert's Reply went to war.

1
ORIGINS

Earlier, on October 10th 1941, at the home of XV Squadron at RAF Wyton in Cambridgeshire, a small yet far reaching event had taken place.

Over a year had passed since the stamp of Nazi control had been embossed over much of continental Europe, from Denmark and Norway through the Low Countries and deep into France. It seemed that only Britain and the Empire stood against the might of Nazi Germany and Italy.

The events of the spring of 1940 had shaken the British military establishment to the core. General Guderian and his blitzkrieg in May 1940 demonstrated to the shocked British Expeditionary Force just what a truly mechanised army could achieve. The British were left standing. The small supporting force of Battles and Blenheims were completely outclassed by the Luftwaffe. Following the miraculous withdrawal of British troops at Dunkirk, the remains of the staff of the army bases and RAF ground crew made their way to Nantes and to the former liner, the Lancastria. Aircrew crammed the lower decks and stood no chance when, just out of port, the ship was attacked and sank with the loss of 3,000, mostly RAF.

Back in England, bedraggled troops were billeted around the country, as the army began to replace the weapons that had been left behind, and prepare itself for invasion. The country was under blackout. Further mass evacuation of children from the cities had been made and everywhere anti- aircraft batteries were being manned day and night. It was an island under siege.

Bomber Command was coming to grips with the reality that its existing heavy bombers, Wellingtons and Hampdens, were only just adequate for the job and the lighter Blenheims were hopelessly susceptible to Luftwaffe attack. Daylight bombing raids exposed aircraft to attack from anti-aircraft flak and fighters, and night raids exposed the inadequacy of navigation unsupported by radio or radar. Nevertheless, day by day bombers took off to drop bombs on airfields in France, on German shipping and on the places in the low countries where invasion preparations were being made and, night after night, on Germany itself. The bombing though was hopelessly inaccurate with few hits on or near target. Most tragic was the loss of life. Crews would be sent into action only partly trained. At one point in 82 Squadron[1] no one knew how many operations had to be flown to complete a tour because no one had survived that long.

The Battle of Britain had been fought and won at the cost of the lives of a great many young fighter pilots. It had also cost the lives and homes of the ordinary men, women and children who had been caught by the bombs of the Luftwaffe in London but also in Liverpool and other cities. Most critically to the war effort, Coventry, where factories had been turning out anything from motor vehicles to aircraft parts, had been devastated on November 14th 1940.

The Battle of the Atlantic was underway at its own cost of a great many merchant seamen, and men of the Royal Navy, as they struggled to bring essential supplies to this island. In North Africa the British under General Wavell had pushed the Italians out of Libya but then Field Marshall Rommel and his Desert Rats had driven the British back to their defensive line in the east.

On June 22nd 1941 Germany had invaded Russia, and Prime Minister Churchill was adamant that Britain should go to their aid supplying tanks and other armaments. This would impose yet another strain on the British war machine. The war was not going well.

Prime Minister Churchill was convinced that victory would only come if Germany itself could be attacked and defeated. He could see no prospect of an invasion unless America could be persuaded to join the war. Some other means were needed. The Air Staff had long been arguing that they had the means

to do this, by attacking Germany from the air and dropping vast quantities of explosive on its factories, its means of
communication and, most controversially, its cities. Yet,
if Bomber Command was to bring the war to Germany it
would need aircraft of sufficient size and power to carry many
tons of explosive.

In the aftermath of the Great War many voices had been
raised against the use of aerial bombardment altogether. No
fewer than three significant attempts were made to reach
international agreement banning bombing from the air. The
reality though was that the genie was well and truly out of the
bottle, and warfare through bombing from the air was a reality
from which the world could not escape. That though wasn't
an end to the matter; debate raged on over just how bombers
should be used.

The view of the German military establishment was, at
least initially, that they were tactical weapons to be deployed
in support of the highly mechanised army. The Luftwaffe nevertheless had gone on to attack airfields, factories and cities
from the air in preparation for the intended German invasion
of Britain. The Battle of Britain put pay to that, but the con-
cept of air attack was very much set in the agenda.

In spite of the public pronouncements of the Baldwin government, a certain amount of rearmament activity had been
going on since the mid-1930s, possibly most crucially as a
network of shadow factories put in place to reduce depen-
dence on existing factories manufacturing aircraft. Sir Wil-

Mk1 Short Stirling

liam Rootes had been approached whilst away with his eldest son on a tour of the Far East. Lord Nuffield had been very proactive in seeking to support rearmament, and his companies played their part most particularly in setting up a repair organisation for crashed fighter planes. The Austin Motor company had dedicated part of their plant at Longbridge to the construction of bombers[2] and there were many more.

A highly significant development came from the realisation that bombing using existing two-engine aircraft was inefficient. What was needed was an aeroplane that could carry three times the weight than could a Wellington. The first of these, which entered service in August 1940, was the Stirling built by Shorts at their plant in Rochester in Kent and based on their highly successful seaplane the Sunderland. The Stirling would be supplemented by the Halifax and the Manchester with its illustrious successor, the Lancaster.

The Stirling was born because of a need by the RAF to introduce a long range heavy bomber, capable of carrying up to 14,000lb bomb loads, and being able to strike deep into enemy territory. No other aircraft before it was capable of satisfying this requirement, and left the country exposed as war seemed inevitable in the second half of the 1930s. The Stirling was based on a four-engined layout of just over 99ft wing span, with a length of 87ft for the fuselage.

Originally the design specification had included a larger wing, but that had been overruled by the Air Ministry and would have seriously altered its flying performance from what had been intended, as the larger wing would not allow the Stirling to fit within the RAF's largest hanger. Even empty the aircraft would weigh over 20 tons, but with its bomb load and 2250 gallons of fuel, with its 'clipped' wings producing less lift than the original design. This would be a major factor in its maximum ceiling height of just about 17,000ft.

The Stirling was powered by four Bristol Hercules engines, each capable of producing 1600hp. These gave the Stirling a top flying speed of around 270mph depending on weather conditions and bomb load. Each engine was supercharged, and cooling was by natural airflow over the engines. One of the problems encountered with the engines was in the servic-

The Short Stirling was such a large aircraft that it presented unique challenges for the ground crews during routine servicing.

ing by ground crews. With the tail down the Stirling's nose was nearly 23ft from the ground, so care was needed to avoid falling from the wings during routine maintenance!

None of this development came without cost. By the end of 1940 Britain's gold reserves were nearly exhausted and it was only saved by the determination of President Roosevelt to obtain the agreement of Congress to the Lend Lease Act in March 1941 which enabled the provision of vital supplies. More was needed though and the government initiated a number of schemes to encourage the British people to give or invest in the war effort. National Savings were promoted by towns and organisations to encourage their citizens to invest in the war effort. One such scheme in the summer of 1941 was the Spitfire Week held in cities around the country, and which paralleled Salute the Soldier weeks and Warship weeks.

There were also individual initiatives. Following the bombing of Coventry, Sir William Rootes, co- founder of the motor group that produced Humber, Hillman, Sunbeam and Singer Cars and Commer and Karrier lorries, persuaded other leaders of the motor industry to give enough to equip a whole Squadron of Spitfires.

There was one initiative which perhaps stood alone, and it was this that led to the event at RAF Wyton on October 10th 1941. On July 31st the Secretary of State for Air, Sir Archibald Sinclair, received a letter from a Lady MacRobert together with a cheque for £25,000 (£700,000 in today's money) to be used to buy a Stirling bomber for the RAF. This astonishing gift had come about because of a conversation Lady MacRobert had had with her third son, Iain, in Spitfire Week in Aberdeen on his most recent leave.

Rachel MacRobert came from a wealthy American family. Her father, William Workman, was a physician from New England. In 1911 she became the second wife of widower Alexander 'Mac' MacRobert, a Scot with substantial interests in India.

Mac came from a working class background, born in the shadow of the Broadford Mill in Aberdeen, one of the many producing high quality woollen textiles that were exported around the world. Two weeks after his birth, so the record goes, the family moved to a croft close to another mill, this time manufacturing paper. Mac went to work at the mill as a sweeper at the age of 12. Stoney Wood Paper Mills were also renowned worldwide, as 'one of the greatest industrial establishments of its time'[3]. As a young man Mac had clearly been determined to make something of his life. He studied at the recently created School of Science and Arts in Aberdeen and went on from there to evening classes at Robert Gordon's College. Soon he was teaching as well.

On December 31st 1883 he married Georgina Porter, a local girl, and headed out to India to a job as a chemist at the Muir Mill in Cawnpore. Georgina was left behind until Mac had established himself. Cawnpore was known as the Manchester of India and, although still bearing the scars of the Indian mutiny some twenty years earlier, it was definitely the right place for an ambitious young man. Mac's renowned determination was put into play the moment he landed, since the chemist's job had already been filled!

He was sent instead to the Cawnpore Woollen Mills and quickly made his mark. It seems he never looked back. Business success came through hard work and fair treatment of his workers; social success came through Georgina's homemaking skills and engaging personality.

Georgina missed Scotland and soon the couple bought the small estate of Douneside within a mile of the village of

Tarland near Aberdeen. This began Mac's journey to becoming a stalwart of the Scottish establishment. Happiness was destined not to last though. Following a long battle with cancer, Georgina died on 30th November 1905. Mac put his efforts into building his businesses into the substantial British India Corporation.

Rachel Workman was many years Mac's junior and was a significant woman in her own right. With both of her parents also being noted Himalayan explorers, she was probably always destined to be adventurous. Although American by birth, she studied Geology at Edinburgh University and Imperial College London. Later she went on to publish several geological works. In 1911 she married Mac and they had three sons. Rachel became a fellow of the Geological Societies of London and Stockholm. If this was not enough, she took to the farming activities of the MacRobert's family and became President of the British Friesian Cattle Society and Royal Northern Agricultural Society.

Mac died on June 22nd 1922 and the eldest son, Alasdair, succeeded to the title. The lad was only aged ten and went on to school at Oundle and then to Cambridge. After university, Alasdair followed his father's footsteps out to India and worked for the British India Corporation whose interests now included cotton and leather in addition to wool; in time, he took over as chairman. His real passions though were for fast cars and aeroplanes.

Lady MacRobert who donated £25,000
to the RAF after the death of her sons for
the purchase of the Stirling that became the
MacRobert's Reply.

Alasdair MacRobert was a man of the 1930s. He was inspired by technology. He drove cars at Donnington Park and
Koblenz in Germany. He was banned for dangerous driving
and speeding. It wasn't only motors cars. In 1935 he learnt
to fly and he clocked up many hours whilst carrying out his
duties for the BIC. In 1937 he founded an aeroplane business
in India. His idea would not seem out of place in the 21st
century service economy: his company, The Indian Aviation
Development Company, would provide aircraft, pilots and
mechanics to fly their customers anywhere in the world. The
company was highly regarded and was offering advice to a
number of Indian states.

Tragedy struck though, and on June 1st 1938 the aeroplane
that he was flying crashed near Luton Airport in Bedfordshire.
He had only recently returned from India to look at expand-
ing his aviation business in Britain.

The Aberdeen Journal of June 2nd 1938 reported that
at Douneside and Cromar, tenants and estate workers were
mourning the death of their 'popular young laird'. The paper
went on to explain that Alasdair's coming-of-age celebrations
in 1933 that went on for two days 'showed the good feelings
between the young laird and his tenantry and workers'. The
Aberdeen Journal in 1933 carried a report on the two-day
party. It seems that he was showered with gifts paid for by
subscription but presented by Lord Aberdeen as Lord Lieutenant of the county but also a close neighbour. It was from

Lord Aberdeen that in 1918 Mac had acquired the Cromar part of his estate.

Lady MacRobert's second son Roderick succeeded to the title. He too had a passion for all things modern as well as being a gifted musician. The Aberdeen Journal reported that he had played at Alasdair's big party. He was studying in Salzburg just before the war and wrote: 'I consider that all the recent behavior (of the Nazis) is high handed, unreasonable and completely unworthy of modern civilisation. I'd rather live in Russia.'

He wanted to follow his brother out to India, but it seems his mother dissuaded him and instead he was commissioned as a Pilot Officer in the RAF in May 1938. He had also gone up to Cambridge following school at Cranleigh. He was sent to out to Egypt where, after Service Flying School, he joined a bomber squadron in Palestine. Here, with the rank of acting Flight Lieutenant, he was awarded the Palestine medal for his service during the Arab revolt. Clearly he was well thought of and soon was appointed adjutant to Air Vice Marshall Arthur Harris who then had command of the RAF in Palestine and Transjordan. When Harris returned to England just before the outbreak of war, Roderick came with him. He was promoted to Flying officer in September 1940.

Given his passion for flying, it was hardly surprising that he found that this administrative role was not for him. So in

May 1941 he moved to lead a group of Hurricanes in action in Iraq to put down the Iraqi revolt. On May 22nd 1941, by then a veteran of the Middle East, he led an attack on the Mosul airbase where many Messerschmitts and Junkers were destroyed.

In a report on the action, the pilot of another Hurricane described the attack: "When we arrived over Mosul, MacRobert dived down to make an attack. Almost at once, his fire set alight two lorries laden with petrol. These went up with a dickens of a flash. Then I came down and we both strafed hangars and aircraft on the ground. I saw MacRobert come down in a second dive and turn away from the attack, but after

Hurricanes in action in the Middle East

that, I never saw him again. Although we are not certain of this, we think he must have been shot down on his way back.

"Our raid was made primarily against Junkers 52s and ME109s as well as Iraqi rebel aircraft on the aerodrome. We were also after German ground personnel and anti-air-craft gun positions. Only when the revolt was over did we find out how successful the raid had been. Large numbers of Junkers and Messerschmitts were found riddled with machine-gun bullets and we also learned that some German pilots were killed by MacRobert in that daring dive, when he went head-long into the enemy."

This is Lady MacRobert and her three sons in happier times before the sons were lost in tragic circumstances.

Rachel's response on hearing of his death was to say: "I am proud to think he did his duty, and carried out so well the spirit of our family motto – Virtuus Gloria Merce (Glory is the reward of valour)". Roderick's remains were later received and buried in Mosul War Cemetery.

It was now the turn of the youngest son, Iain, to take the MacRobert's title. He too was flying mad and, when war was declared, had joined the RAF Volunteer Reserve in the ranks and was commissioned on November 3rd 1940 as a Pilot Officer. After training at the School of General Reconnaissance, he joined Coastal Command. There he flew twenty-five operational flights escorting convoys and carrying out daylight reconnoiters over Denmark and Norway.

On June 30th 1941 Iain was posted missing after an operation in which he flew a Blenheim to search for a bomber thought to have ditched over Flamborough Head. Ten men in two dinghies were rescued but no sign could be found of the fourth and last Baronet of Cawnpore and Cromar. His name is remembered on the Air Forces Memorial at Runnymede near Windsor.

Rachel MacRobert was then not only a widow, but had lost her three sons whom she had brought up almost single handed. It must have seemed that Hitler was having it all his own way. Rachel MacRobert was made of sterner stuff though, and resolved that the MacRoberts would have their reply, as is crystal clear in her letters to Sir Archibald Sinclair:

"It is my wish to make a mother's immediate reply in the way that I know would also be my boys' reply; attacking, striking sharply, straight to the mark – the gift of £25,000 – to buy a bomber to carry on their work in the most effective way. This expresses my reaction on receiving the news about my sons.

"I am proud to read what you say about their work. I never doubted but that they would do their duty. I very much appreciate your personal expression of sympathy at this time. I can only hope that my youngest son may yet return.

"In any case they would be glad that their mother replied for them, and helped to strike a blow at the enemy. So I feel that a suitable name for the bomber would be 'MacRobert's Reply'. Might it carry the MacRobert Crest – two fronds of bracken, with hand grasping an Eastern Crown? Or simply our Badge – a frond of bracken and an Indian Rose crossed?

"Let it be used where it is most needed – Coastal Command for preference. May good fortune go with those who fly it. I should like to know (confidentially) where it serves, and if it succeeds in doing anything of special note. I would also appreciate a photograph of it for my records (private).

"I have no more sons to wear the Badge, or carry it in the fight. My eldest son Sir Alasdair, was killed when his own plane crashed in a strange way, soon after he had flown home from India. He had been held up in Italy for three weeks during Hitler's visit there in 1938. Sir Roderick was the third Baronet, and joined the RAF in 1938. Iain, my youngest,

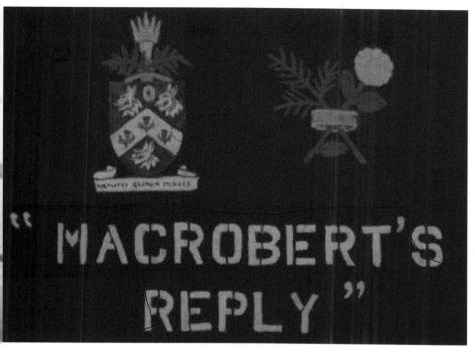

A replica of the MacRobert's Reply nose art by Farlam Airframes

would be the fourth Baronet. None of them ever looked for the easy way. If I had ten sons, I know they would all have followed that line of duty.

"It is with a mother's pride that I enclose my cheque for £25,000 – and with it goes my sympathy to those mothers who have also lost sons, and gratitude to all mothers who sons gallantly carry on the fight."

As only recently bereaved she didn't want to be interviewed by the press, but she did agree to an interview that would then be put out by the Press Association. The text of that interview is in the archive. When you read it you realise that there are quotes attributed to her which tell much of this remarkable woman.

She begins: "my gift was decided on in a flash...the idea was born when the signal came from the Air Ministry telling me that my youngest son, Iain, was missing and I took my decision there and then."

Continuing, she says, "Both my sons showed signs of brilliant promise. They had everything in their favour to help them – a substantial education, training on highly specialised lines, rather original and unusual, and a considerable knowledge of men and affairs, assisted by wide travel. But it was not to be. Whatever the future now holds for me I am determined to strike wherever possible and whenever possible to end the curse of our world today – this curse which our great Prime Minister has called "the evil thing".

"You already know that I have no one left to carry on the fight and the next best thing is to see that other mothers' sons are supplied with the finest weapons with which to wage the struggle. Naturally my first interest is in the Air Force – that fine service which has already done so much for the country. I hope that my aircraft MacRobert's Reply will be able to strike many shrewd, well aimed, and powerful blows at the enemy. I am glad that a 'Stirling' bomber is being bought with my gift. The name 'Stirling' has a fine Scottish flavour with a warlike history in past days and now."

What struck me most was her vehemence against Germany. She says of the Nazi regime: "This must end. I have known since early girlhood when even then I was a rebel against their system. They have made a practice of fighting their wars outside their own country and they evidently hope to do the same this time. They miscalculated the power of the Royal Air Force and our boys, as they have failed to understand the spirit of our people. Peace loving – yes – but *how* we can all fight. The Mothers will all have their own way, too, of showing what they can do. It is dangerous to rouse such a spirit. There is nothing pleases me more than to hear the Air Ministry communiques announcing the increasing number and volume of raids on all parts of Germany. 'Strike them hard and strike them often,' must be our watchword.

"In my sorrow today, I think of those other mothers who have lost their near and dear ones. Ours is a proud sorrow (as the Queen has said in her Broadsheet) and I feel that we must not break faith with those who have laid down their lives and made the complete sacrifice for what must be the greatest cause men have ever fought and died for. To be truly worthy of such sacrifices we must carry on – all of us – to make the world a better place for all freedom loving men and women. To attain that end we must all be workers, however long the burden must be carried, and whatever the cost."

Many of these quotes found their way into the press. There is a letter in the archive from Rachel MacRobert telling of the huge response she'd received from mothers everywhere. Cleary she had caught the mood of the time.

The official presentation of the first MacRobert's Reply N6086 to Squadron Leader Boggis in 1941

At the ceremony at RAF Wyton on October 10th 1941, the CO of XV Squadron, Wing Commander Ogilvie, entrusted the MacRobert's Reply Stirling, N6086 call sign LS - F, to its first skipper Flying Officer Peter Boggis, encouraged by these words from her ladyship: "The best of good luck boys, always, and whenever and wherever you go. I know you will strike hard, sharp, and straight to the mark. That is the only language the enemy understands. My thoughts and those of thousands of other mothers are with you, and we are truly grateful to all concerned. Also thanks to those of you who have the care of my 'Reply' and prepare her for her flights. May the blows you strike bring us nearer victory. God bless you all."

The aircraft had the MacRobert coat of arms painted on to its nose, and was given the code LS-F, LS being the squadron code and the last letter identifying the aircraft as "F for Freddie", a designation all subsequent aircraft given the name MacRobert's Reply have used.

The Stirling was standard Mark B1 although this particular aircraft was more probably manufactured at the Shorts factory in Belfast, Rochester having suffered at the hand of the Luftwaffe. Sandie Craven-Griffith recalls that her father had worked at the Rochester factory and had been moved to factory near Gloucester, so N 6086 F may well have been manufactured there rather than Belfast.

This is what she says: "My father was Marias George Percy West – known throughout his life and to all relatives and friends as "Jock". He was born September 14th, 1913, and entered the Royal Navy as an artificer about 1928 or 1929. He was invalided out because of an attack of pleurisy that marked his lungs.

"Because of the marked lungs, Jock was unable to join the armed forces, but he found employment with Short Brothers in Rochester, working 'on the bench', building the Stirling bomber. Short Brothers had developed the Sunderland Flying Boat in the thirties, using the River Medway as the runway. It was now 1940 and Chatham/Rochester was the last line of AA defence before London and Jock was working sometimes around the clock. The factory was bombed in the autumn of 1940 and Short Brothers and the Stirling production facilities moved to Gloucester."

1   Bomber Command, Max Hastings loc 1147
2   Stirling Wings - the Short Stirling goes to War, Jonathan Falconer, Sutton Publishing, Stroud, 1995, 1997, 26
3   Miller loc 132

2
OPERATIONS

Peter Boggis always said that he couldn't understand why he had been chosen to fly the Reply, since he had understood that Lady MacRobert had wanted a Scot[4] and Boggis had been born in Barnstable. Lady MacRobert had been told that no promises about the pilot could be made since, 'the days of one aircraft, one crew are over'. Boggis was very experienced by then, with over 60 operations under his belt. He'd been a policeman with the Met and had accepted a short service commission with the RAF in June 1937. He'd been promoted to Flying Officer in May 1941 and posted to XV Squadron on June 6th 1941. Immediately he was flying Stirlings having previously flown Wellingtons in 38 Squadron.

The other members of that first MacRobert crew included 'Red' King as second pilot and Buck Ryan as navigator. 'Red'

King had been in the timber trade before enlisting in the volunteer reserve back in May 1939. John (Buck) Ryan was one
of a great many young men from the Dominions who joined
that RAF. He was a New Zealander from Timaru and older
at age 30. He was married and had travelled to the U.S. to
study and, when he had completed the course, his wife joined
him and they both worked for Bernar McFadden in Dansville,
New York. It was whilst he was at Dansville that he learned to
fly. When war broke out, they waited for their son (John Jr) to
be born and then tried to get a booking for mother and son to
return to New Zealand. Being war time, this took some time,
but they finally secured a cabin on the Port Hunter. After
their departure, John Ryan travelled to Canada to enlist in the
Royal Canadian Air Force. He joined 11 Operational Training
Unit from June 27th 1941, and finally joined XV Squadron
on August 1st 1941[5].

The other crew members were Sgt Watson flight engineer, Sgt Wilson rear gunner, Sgt Gould mid-upper gunner,
Sgt Clark front gunner and Sgt Allen wireless officer. Watson
was a Scot who'd enlisted straight from school. Wilson had
been a labourer, Gould had worked at Woolworths as an
assistant manager, Clark had been an accounts clerk and Allen
an electrician. In only a few months, second pilot 'Red' King
would be replaced by New Zealander Sergeant Higgins, and
Allen and Clark by Sergeants Mountenay and Butterworth[6].

The first operation flown by N6086 was on October 12th
1941 to Nuremberg[7]. These men were each 'one of the many',

as indeed were the MacRobert brothers: young men from different parts of Great Britain and the Dominions and from different echelons in society. As the likelihood of war had grown in the late 1930s young men like these had found themselves faced with a dreadful choice. The memories of the carnage of trench warfare were still vivid; the young men had fathers, many of whom had died or were living with their wounds. Hardly a family in the land had not lost at least one member. The prospect of it happening all over again was chilling. This was a large part of the picture. The other was what had so attracted the MacRobert brothers.

In the Britain of the 1930s, when much of the country was wracked by economic depression, there were areas of growth. The motor car manufacturers were producing ever more enticing models and these were being bought be a growing cross section of the population. Young men and fast cars seems almost a cliché, but it was true: many were addicted 'petrol boots'. It has been said more than once that the experience of driving fast cars greatly sharpened the reactions and this had a direct and positive benefit on pilots particularly in the Battle of Britain. Those who couldn't afford fast cars dreamt of driving them, and many of them and those who actually drove the cars dreamt of flying aeroplanes. There was the attraction of adventure and risk. Of course those who loved the sea were drawn to the navy, but for other adventure seekers, sadly for the army where the memory of the trenches was too close, volunteering for the RAF was in a sense the obvious choice. It was so 'obvious' that throughout the war the RAF had more volunteers for aircrew than they could possibly handle.

Volunteers were subjected to a rigorous selection process and this was followed by demanding general training. At this point volunteers would be selected for particular roles. Many with aspirations to fly fighters were frequently disappointed as they were directed toward bombers, seen as cumbersome 'heavy lorries' when compared to the nimble 'sports car' of the fighter. Of those selected for bombers there would be pilots, navigators, wireless operators and gunners. Flight engineers would often first have been ground crew or working for manufacturers; they would have engineering backgrounds. Many months of specialist training would follow, often in the Dominions in order to benefit from better weather. The freshly trained would come together in Operational Training Units where they would, largely it seemed by self-selection, form themselves into crews.

This 'crewing up' was an inspired idea that probably saved many lives and helped to ensure that crews worked as a team. Unlike a fighter, where it was all down to the pilot, the essential roles in a Stirling were divided between the, normally, seven crew members. The pilot, whether or not he was commissioned, was the leader. He gave instructions and carried responsibility; in particular, he had to be the last man out. Although 'Red' King was initially second pilot, this role had largely gone by 1941. It had been found to be largely unnecessary but it also meant that the number of operations were unduly limited. The pilot, though, could not possibly operate without the other crew members.

The pilot and crew once airborne was often a contrast with the same men on the base. Many of these bases dating back to the 1920s would house solid career NCOs, many of whom resented deeply the young Flight Sergeants who came in as newly trained aircrew. The impact of the resentment would grow to a pitch where different messes had to be provided for the non-commissioned aircrew. The segregation of officers was even sharper, with those from public schools and university enjoying the best accommodation, food and drink and being looked after by a batman. These distinctions, however, rapidly disappeared once crews were airborne.

At a time when this country was facing its darkest hours, it had called upon its young men to stand to the line. They did so in their thousands with amazing bravery at such a young age. A great number of these enlisted in the RAF, many of whom then joined Bomber Command. They would learn all too soon that the reality of being a bomber crew was very far removed from any romantic notions they may have had.

Some of these young men became aircrew in XV Squadron. Just a handful of these would become the crew of the famous MacRobert's Reply. They soon became friends who faced danger together in many missions. Unfortunately all but one would be lost.

From May 1940 until August 1942, XV Squadron was based at RAF Wyton in Cambridgeshire. Peter Boggis quite obviously liked it:

"Wyton was a nice station with good pubs in the area of St Ives and Huntingdon, and Cambridge within striking distance. Cambridge in those days was a bright city and the Mecca for all aircrew within a reasonable radius. Every 'night out' was a virtual reunion with our chums.

Wyton was fairly easy to find from the air because of two parallel canals that ran from the Wash almost to Huntingdon – a great asset when returning from 'ops' in cloudy weather. These canals were also part of our official low flying area. Looking back, we must have frightened no end of farmers, locals and cattle with our Stirlings roaring over their heads only a few feet up[8]."

At the beginning of the war many of the aerodromes at which the Squadrons were stationed comprised solid buildings put up in the 1920s and 1930s, a far cry from the Nissen huts that would house crews on the makeshift airfields that would in time cover much of eastern England. Wyton was one such solid aerodrome.

On January 21st 1942, Lady MacRobert was sent a short report[9] of the activities of the MacRobert's Reply. This also marked the occasion of the award of the DFC to the pilot, Flying Officer Boggis. The report tells how the MacRobert's Reply first went into action on the 29th September 1941, when the aircraft took part in a long-distance raid on the Baltic port of Stettin, which was being used by the Germans to support their Russian front. It adds that the flying time for the trip was 8 hours 10 minutes[10].

The report continues: In October the MacRobert's Reply was out on five nights. First there were raids on Nuremberg; one on October 10th[11] and another four nights later[12]. Attacks on Bremen and Brest followed on October 20th and 24th respectively. All of these were night raids. Then on October 28th the Captain and crew of MacRobert's Reply were detailed for another long-distance raid. In this attack the aircraft was damaged by enemy action and was under repair for some weeks.

"The trip was a nightmare from start to finish", said the pilot, "there was very bad weather all over Europe. We got in the vicinity of the target but could not see anything. We got hit several times – over the coast, over the target, and on the way back."

The next operation was on the night of December 11/12th when the target was Cologne. Four nights later MacRobert's Reply was over Brest where the German warships, the Gneisnau and Scharnhorst, were in dry dock. Then on December 18th (Anniversary of the Wellington's epic fight with German fighters in the Helgoland Bight two years previously) Bomber Command sent a mixed force of heavy bombers – Stirlings, Halifaxes and Manchesters – into Brest in daylight after the ships. The Stirlings led the way, and flying in one of the Stirling formations was MacRobert's Reply.

Describing this raid, the Captain said, "We were attacked five times by fighters. Just before we got to the target, one dived on us from out of the sun. He attacked us twice and the second time we reckon we got him. He went over on his back and dived straight down. We went on and bombed. Our bombs fell very close to, if not on, one of the ships. We were attacked again by fighters after bombing and just after we crossed the French coast."

Once again the aircraft was put temporarily hors de combat but it was back in service again on January 10th and at Hamburg four nights later. Peter Boggis had mixed feelings about the Stirling: "My memory of the Stirling aircraft was of a huge aeroplane with the pilot's cockpit a long way off the ground, due to the massive undercarriage that created a lot of drag, especially with a full load on board. It had a very poor heating system and an operating height that compared very unfavourably with that of Halifaxes' or Lancasters'. However, once airborne, with the undercarriage safely up, I found the aircraft pleasant to fly and quite manoeuvrable. Fortunately it could also take a lot of punishment from flak[13]."

The Operation Record Book shows that the attack on Brest was the last flight in the MacRoberts for Peter Boggis and from then on it was 'Red' King who captained the aircraft. The composition of the crew also changed with Don Jeffs taking over as wireless operator, with Len Gornall as Flight engineer, a Canadian named Charbonneau, and Sergeants Harry Meads, Clark, Kennedy and Long.

Wireless operator Don Jeffs had been born in December 1920 in Sawley just outside the former lace-making town of Long Eaton near Nottingham. On leaving school he had worked for the Long Eaton Co-op. His passion, though, was radio. Many, possibly most, of those young men who volunteered for the RAF did so because, like the MacRobert brothers, they were attracted by flying; for Don it was because he could actually work with his passion for wireless there. He had been in the scouts and had gained his Signals Badge and was proficient both in Morse Code and Semaphore.

He had volunteered for aircrew in 1940 and was sent away to Cardington until there was a training place available. This came in the winter of 1940 when he was sent to Blackpool for intensive training with Marconi, which, he remembered, was significantly better than the RAF's own training in wireless. His existing proficiency at Morse may have helped him leap-frog other wireless operator volunteers who could be found in halls all over the town labouring to master this vital skill[14]. His training with Marconi included not only how to operate the radio but also how to repair it and indeed how it worked; Ohm's law became almost a standing joke[15].

The role of wireless operator combined the operation of radio with a technical proficiency in electronics generally. Don was in his element. Less attractive was the bitter cold of that winter and the drill that all had to undertake. Following a further advanced course he was posted first to Lossiemouth, Scotland and then, in May 1941, to RAF Wyton to await a gunnery course; wireless operators had to double up as gunners on occasions. He was posted to 3 Group Training Flight at Newmarket Heath.

In September 1941, he returned to Wyton and flew Stirlings initially as member of Flight Lieutenant Ryall's crew, but also with other crews when they were in need of a proficient wireless operator. Such was the attrition rate that many crews had men missing through injury or death and any aircrew with specialist experience were much sought after to fill the ranks. Fortunately for Don he was asked to 'crew-up' as a member of Flying Officer 'Red' King's crew and he flew many missions with them. When F/O King had to step down due to ear trouble, his crew were 'adopted' by Squadron Leader John Hall and their permanent association with N6086 F, the MacRobert's Reply was established and friendships were formed.

Len Gornall was Don Jeff's closest chum in the Squadron. He was a flight engineer. Len was one of the men who would go for rides in Don's Sunbeam sports car. The story behind the Sunbeam sheds a little light on some of the reality of life in a bomber squadron. Don had made the highest bid in an auction of the effects of a member of the Squadron who had failed to return from an operation; he was presumed dead. Any belongings of the deceased that the next of kin did not want would be auctioned and the proceeds would be sent to the next of kin.

Don recalled driving the Sunbeam with an impossible number of passengers: fellow crew members and WAAFs from

Sgt Donald Jeffs in 1941

A pencil drawing of the young and older Donald Jeffs by Rosie Rockets. It was presented to Donald by Roger Leivers (Godmanchester Stirling) at the 2016 Godmanchester Veterans Day event.

Wyton. They would visit local pubs including the Golden Lion in St Ives (which was the favoured watering hole for young airmen from the various RAF bases in the area), and the Pike & Eel by the river[16]. Don recalls one particular trip with Len when they drove right over to Birkenhead to visit Len's sister who worked at the Argyle Theatre which hosted many of the famous music hall acts of the time[17].

Len later joined 138 Squadron flying from RAF Tempsford on SOE duties. He had been promoted to Flying Officer and had received the DFC after surviving a crash of a Halifax during his 48th operation, and evading capture with the help of the local resistance. Whilst with 138 Squadron he was listed as missing on February 26th 1945 with the rest of his crew after the loss of his aircraft over the North Sea. After the war Don Jeffs always wondered what had happened to his pal, but it was not until 2015 that Len's fate became known. Although saddened to hear of his friend's loss, especially so close to the end of the war, Don was assured that Len had not simply forgotten him.

When not drafted onto the MacRobert's Reply crew Len Gornall was often crewed up with Squadron Leader Drummond Wilson who had been in the RAF in the 30s and then rejoined once war was declared. He joined XV Squadron as a Squadron Leader in October 1941. Sqn Ldr Wilson and his crew, although based at RAF Wyton, had been operating from nearby RAF Alconbury, which had better runways, when they took off in Stirling N3703 on April 10th 1942 to bomb Essen in Germany. The aircraft was badly damaged by anti-aircraft fire during the attack and turned for home.

Crew members managed to coax the crippled Stirling back to Alconbury and were about to land when they were forced to abort the landing because other aircraft were on the runway despite instructions from controllers. Squadron Leader Wilson carried out another circuit, but as the bomber banked a damaged oil pipe broke and both starboard engines seized, causing the aircraft to crash near Rectory Farm and Cow Lane in Godmanchester.

Squadron Leader Wilson was killed in the crash, along with mid-upper gunner Sergeant Edgar Gould. Other crew members were thrown clear, but injured Flying Officer Clifford Reeve went back into the burning wreckage to rescue two colleagues and won a commendation[18].

Sgt Edgar Gould who was killed in the Godmanchester crash had often crewed in the N6086 MacRobert's Reply under Flying Officer King, and was therefore known to Don Jeffs. In fact he had not been due to fly in N3703 but replaced the normal crew gunner, Sgt Johnnie Spalding, who was receiving treatment for frostbite from a previous operation. As often happened during wartime, the way this unscheduled change occurred resulted in the worst of outcomes. Ironically Sgt Spalding was himself killed a few months later in September 1942 during an operation to Duisburg with VII Squadron. At an RAF veterans day in Godmanchester in May 2015 organised by Roger Leivers, Don met

Phillippa Kirby the granddaughter of Sgt. Gould. Phillippa was so pleased to be able to talk to someone who had known her grandfather during those difficult times.

At the end of January 1942, Stirlings from XV Squadron were sent up to Lossiemouth to join the attack on the Von Tirpitz which had been found in the Fjords near Trondheim. The Record Book states that it barely stopped raining and snowing the whole time, and so despite several attempts the poor weather soon forced the abandonment of this operation, and the aircraft of XV Squadron were ordered back to Wyton on February 6th. It soon became apparent that the weather would yet again hamper their efforts, and all but one of the aircraft had to divert to nearby Peterhead following icing on the wings.

The MacRobert's Reply, N6086 F with Red King's crew on board, was about to take off but hit a Spitfire, "which shouldn't have been there[19]". Philip Jeffs thinks that the MacRobert's Reply probably caught its wheel in a snowbank on the side of the runway due to heavy crosswinds, and was pulled sideways into a Spitfire most likely left there due to the foul weather the day before. Both aircraft were seriously damaged. All the crew escaped uninjured, but for Sgt 'Duncan' Jeffs this crash was to be the first of two that he would survive in a MacRobert's Reply Stirling. He remembers that one moment he was looking at his radio instrument panel as the takeoff began, and then his port window was full of the left wing and engine. "There was no panic," says Don, "we simply got out and waited in the cold for someone to come and give us a lift". It says much for the fortitude of those young men that the crew of the MacRobert's Reply were passengers on board Stirling 'D' for Donald bound for Wyton within an hour of the crash none the worse for their ordeal.

It seems that care was taken to try to ensure that no one found out that the MacRobert's Reply had ended up so ignominiously. The panel bearing the crest was removed from N6086 F and was placed on the Stirling R9302 F. There was no ceremony this time. It was said that the lorry carrying away the crashed aircraft had been spotted and someone had seen the name MacRobert still on it[20].

The damaged aircraft was taken to the 'miracle factory'. This was the Short Brothers Repair Organisation (SEBRO) and was based on the Madingley Road on the way out of Cambridge[21]. This very large organisation, employing some 4,500 people, many of whom were women, had been set up to recover, repair or re-use parts from damaged Stirlings. Ford-Jones notes that N6086 F was repaired but was written off after crashing through engine failure on March 14th[22]. It is unclear whether it had returned to operations or had been used for training purposes. Notes on the file in the National Archives point to the latter.

Stirling R9302 F now carried the MacRobert crest although it isn't clear that the new aircraft was to bear the name MacRobert's Reply or indeed be flown by any particular crew, although operational records show that Sgt Donald Jeffs flew in it thereby maintaining his own personal connection to the 'MacRobert's Reply'. It was built by Short Brothers and Harland, Belfast and was delivered as LS-F to XV Squadron on the February 5th 1942.

Its first operation to Kiel on February 25th was flown by Flying Officer Barr with his crew of Pilot Officer Young with Sergeants Lawson, Johnson-Biggs, Surridge, Thompson-Horan, and East. On February 27th, Flight Lieutenant Ryall's crew came together and flew R9302 F; the crew comprised Pilot Officers Ryan and Burgess, Sergeants Nicholson, Spriggs, Butterworth, Gould and Lt Young. The target was Kiel but changed to Wilhelmshaven. Wing Commander Mac-

N6086 MacRobert's Reply at Peterhead, Scotland after crashing into a Spitfire on take-off to return to RAF Wyton. The Stirling caught its wheel on a snowbank and slewed sideways into the parked Spitfire. It was the last time that N6086 would carry the MacRobert's Reply name.

Donald piloted the other aircraft on that raid with the crew who had formerly flown with King, including Sgt Jeffs. Red King's crew had continued to fly together until February 23rd which may have been the occasion when King suffered a burst eardrum and had to give up operational flying.

Flying Officer Barr's crew flew R9302 in raids on Essen on March 8th and Hamburg on March 9th. Flight Sergeant Barron took over for Gelsenkirchen on March 10th. There was then a gap in operations because of bad weather until March 23rd, and indeed R9302 did not fly another operation until April 2nd when it went on a raid to Poissy under Flying Officer Barr and again to Cologne on April 5th also under Barr. It was Flight Sergeant Shepherd who was skipper for a raid on Dortmund on April 15th and Pilot Officer Arnott who skippered the Gardening operation to Helgoland on April 17th.

On April 22nd Squadron Leader John Hall took over as skipper on a Gardening operation in the Baltic with a crew of Ryan, Nicholson, Butterworth, Spriggs, Jeffs – who had been serving at 3 Group Training Flight at Newmarket since the end of February – and Sullivan; Frank Sharp wouldn't join the crew until April 25th on Hall's second operation as skipper of R 9302 on a raid to Rostock. R9302 was then piloted by Pilot Officer Barron on a raid to Cologne on April 27th.

R9302 never again appeared in the Operations Record Book after April when, on a raid to Kiel with Flight Sergeant Charbonneau as pilot, it was reported as unable to climb to a sufficient altitude. This was a problem that had dogged Stirlings from the start. The aircraft varied. The Record Book reported the Stirling of Don Jeff's first operation bombing from 17,000 ft. on the raid on Stettin on September 27th 1941, but many other Stirlings had been unable to rise above the flak and so had either arrived home severely damage or not at all. Flying through the Alps en route for Italy was a particular danger for Stirlings with many failing to return[23]. The reason for the difficulty with altitude was put down by Don Jeffs and others to the aircraft's wing span. It was said to have been designed with a span of 102 ft. but that this had had to be reduced to 96 ft. to fit the then largest hangars.

The records show that R9302 was changed to 'Z' on the XV Squadron Conversion Flight on May 5th 1942 but was not finally struck off charge until January 14th 1945[24]. Squadron Leader Hall's crew flew on May 6th to Stuttgart and on May 8th to Warnemunde, each time on different aircraft. This bears out the statement made at the outset that no promises could be made to Lady MacRobert on the same crew always flying the same aircraft.

There is a gap showing no operations after May 8th until May 17th. No reason is given for this gap, although we can infer from subsequent events a third Stirling W7531 was given the MacRobert crest. This aircraft had been manufactured by the Austin Motor Company at Longbridge[25] and had been equipped with the new secret GEE navigation system[26]. Squadron Leader John Hall and his crew of Flying Officer Ryan (navigator), Sergeants Spriggs (Flight engineer),

Nicholson, Butterworth, Sharp (gunners) and Jeffs (wireless operator) had been designated to fly W7531 on its maiden operation of 'Gardening' – dropping mines off Denmark.

On May 17th Flying Officer Booth had arrived on a visit from 20 Operational Training Unit and had asked Hall if he could join the crew of W7531. It seems he wanted to see the effectiveness of the new GEE navigation equipment. A ninth member of the crew was Sergeant Maycock who was a trainee navigator working alongside Buck Ryan.

The GEE navigation system had been introduced to try to address the serious shortcomings in the accuracy of bombing. It was based on a grid of radio signals sent at precisely timed intervals from stations at Daventry, Ventnor, and Stenigot Hill. The signals were received by radio sets on board the aircraft. The differences in timing between the signals was then computed and the location of the aircraft plotted on a cathode ray screen[27].

4   Bomber Squadron - Men who flew with XV, Martyn Ford-Jones, William Klimber, London1987, 47

5   Philip Jeffs

6   National Archives

7   XV Squadron Operations Record Book, the National Archives

8   Bomber Squadron - Men who flew with XV, Martyn Ford-Jones, William Klimber, London1987, 43

9   National Archives

10 The Operation Record Book for XV Squadron reports the raid on Stettin but does not include N6086 amongst the aircraft taking part. Ford-Jones at page 48 also records 12th October as N 6086 first operations

11 The Operation Record Book records the formal handing over of the MacRobert's Reply on 10 October and the raid on Nuremberg on 12 October

12 The Operation Record Book does record a raid on 14 October.

13 Bomber Squadron - Men who flew with XV, Martyn Ford-Jones, William Klimber, London1987, 44

14 Imperial War Museum recording, Bowers   11081/10/1

15 Stirling Wings - the Short Stirling goes to War, Jonathan Falconer, Sutton Publishing, Stroud, 1995, 1997, 51

16 Letter of April 1988 from Don Jeffs to Mr 'Robbie' Roberts in the archive held by Martyn Ford-Jones

17 Philip Jeffs

18 All information regarding the 'Godmanchester Stirling' & crews courtesy of Roger Leivers

19 Don Jeffs on www.lostaircraft.com

20 Oxford's Own Men and machines of No 15/XV Squadron Royal flying Corps/Royal Airforce, 101

21 Stirling Wings - the Short Stirling goes to War, Jonathan Falconer, Sutton Publishing, Stroud, 1995, 1997, 43

22 Bomber Squadron - Men who flew with XV, Martyn Ford-Jones, William Klimber, London1987, 53

23 Stirling Wings - the Short Stirling goes to War, Jonathan Falconer, Sutton Publishing, Stroud, 1995, 1997, 41

24 Alan Fraser, Mildenhall Register

25 Martyn Ford-Jones

26 Philip Jeffs

27 http://www.lancaster-archive.com/bc_gee.htm

3

THE CRASH

On the night of May 17th 1942, MacRobert's Reply was one of approximately sixty bombers that took off from many different RAF bases to take part in mine laying operations in the Danish Sound. The code name for the operation was 'Gardening', and the area for the W7531 to target was the 'Daffodil' region (the southerly entrance to Øresund).

Squadron Leader Hall started the Bristol Hercules engines at 2140. Don Jeffs recalls that the night was clear but moon-less[28]. Their mission that night was to lay six tons of 'vegetable' mines in 'Daffodil', the code name for an area off the Norwegian coast called Øresund. The Stirling was to fly at 3000 feet north east to the southern coast of Norway, then fly south just over the tip of southern Sweden, and then at Malmo to reduce altitude to a few hundred feet and fly due west towards the Jutland peninsula of Denmark to commence the bombing run into the Danish Sound. The method of laying these mines was called 'Gardening', but this would be no leisurely pastime – in a short while all hell itself would break loose.

The outward leg to Norway went smoothly due to the masterly skills of the Kiwi navigator John 'Buck' Ryan who had joined from the Canadian Royal Air Force, and who was nicknamed after the comic strip cartoon of the time. The crew enjoyed the usual in-flight entertainment of local radio stations tuned into the aircraft intercom by the wireless operator Sgt Donald 'Duncan' Jeffs. As they neared the enemy coastline Sgt Jeffs cut the radio transmissions and they maintained radio silence to reduce the possibility of detection.

As they flew down the Swedish southern flank the customary 'assistance' was received from the Swedish army who merely fired a few very low-level anti-aircraft rounds without the slightest intention of showing real aggression, and then crossed their searchlights which was always interpreted to mean 'good luck'. For a neutral country, Sweden always made sure the allied bombers received as much assistance as possible[29].

As the MacRobert's Reply began to turn west towards Denmark, Squadron Leader Hall pushed the stick forward and throttled back the engines in order to reduce speed and altitude for the bombing run. RAF intelligence had indicated that there were no gun batteries positioned on that area of coastline, and that the only other hazards were the batteries on the Danish coast, but the MacRobert's Reply and its crew intended to be flying back westward well before that.

As they descended to 200 feet and prepared to open the bomb bay doors, the roar of heavy guns, and the piercing crash of shrapnel exploding beside the aircraft shattered the peaceful evening. The intelligence report, while correct about the shore batteries, had omitted to include the huge destroyer Prince Eugen anchored in the Sound and now using its anti-aircraft guns at an impossibly large target just 200 feet off the water's surface.

The plane shuddered as the port engine took a direct hit and burst into flames. "Skipper, the port engine's on fire," echoed several of the crew together[30], but Squadron Leader Hall was having his own problems trying to gain steerage and altitude. As the aircraft somehow continued to defy the laws of gravity, it remained fixed on a westerly heading – towards the Danish mainland. The crew desperately tried to jettison the six tons of mines but the control mechanism for the bay doors refused to play its part in the drama, as the huge bomber struggled to stay in the air.

Other smaller moored vessels now added their guns to fire at the huge bomber. Logger 'Hagen' from HSFL Kopenhagen also fired 31 rounds of 2cm and 28 rounds with a machinegun, while Logger 'Königsberg' from the same unit fired 37 rounds of 2cm and 20 rounds with a machinegun. A further 9 rounds of 7.5cm and 160 rounds of 2cm were fired from shore positions as well. MacRobert's Reply was hit several times.

"Skipper, were coming up to the Little Belt bridge, we must try to go round," shouted Buck Ryan, the conversation heard clearly by the person next to him. Sgt Jeffs surveyed the coastline through the huge fire streaking past the window next to his wireless operator's chair on the port side. "Yeah, Buck I know, but I've no controls," the skipper responded. "I'm going to try to get to the North Sea so we can ditch her if we need to". Immediately after the verbal exchange the anti-aircraft batteries on the bridge saw the huge target coming

This is the German anti-aircraft battery situated on the Little Belt Bridge who were credited with shooting down the MacRobert's Reply.

toward them on fire. As the spotlights picked up, W7531 and the crew saw the shadows reflecting from the intense glare in the aircraft's windows, an unnatural silence sat heavily in the plane as their destiny began to take shape.

On the 1Km long bridge over the Little Belt, the Germans had stationed light flak (3./lei Flak Abt. 844). The first barrage of 20mm shells from the guns on the bridge found its mark and the MacRobert's Reply was hit again and again. The plane turned violently to port and dived earthwards, her gallant fight for survival all but over. As the huge aircraft descended, it ploughed through the spruce trees of the Mathilde plantation in Gals Klint Forest. It crashed with a huge explosion that tore a massive rock from the ground and laid waste to over an acre of prime forest. As the once proud bomber broke into many burning pieces that created a firestorm within the dry trees, its young crew completed their last mission in the MacRobert's Reply LS-F.

The following is an excerpt from the personal written history of Niels Ebbed Lundholt, a witness to the crashsite:

"Monday, 18th May 1942, I heard rumours that an English bomber was crashed in the Hindsgavl forest, and I took my bicycle and went to the area, in order to see if I could find some weapons I could use against the Germans. I brought a Kodak box camera, in case that I could retrieve any useful informations.

At the crash site, a big part of the forest was cut, it almost looked like a huge razor had cut through the trees.

It looked like there had been a huge explosion, since there were only small parts left from the bomber and there was a big hole in the ground. I could not recognise the bomber.

There were a mixture of German soldiers and Danish people at the site, so I was hiding my camera in a bag in a way so I could take some photos, without anybody noticed it. I did not find any weapons, but I found parts of the radio, a pressure vessel, parts of the attitude meter and the navigation system, which I brought with me.

At a later stage, I spoke with a Danish soldier, who claimed that he had been talking to the only survivor, one of the "gunners", who told him that the aeroplane was about to make an emergency landing and had the landing lights on, when the air defence guns at the Lillebælt bridge shot down the plane. I was shocked over this terrible and barbaric act, but not surprised".

Don Jeffs' son, Philip, later made extensive enquiries about the crash. This is what he discovered: The German military arrived at the crash scene at 02.30hrs and quickly enlisted the 'help' of the local fire service that had already arrived at the site under the supervision of the Chief Fire Officer Jensen. C/O Jensen organised his teams into two parties. The first would fight the fire raging around the wreckage and threatening the surrounding forest. The second 'Falck' (salvage) team would find anything at the crash scene that could identify the plane and its crew, and would remove the bodies for later

SERGEANT D. JEFFS, R.A.F.,
Younger son of Mr. and Mrs. B. C.
Jeffs, of 20, Mayfield-grove, Long
Eaton, who is reported "missing."

*A report in the Nottingham Evening News that Sgt
Donald Jeffs was missing following the crash of the
MacRobert's Reply. It was assumed at that point that
he was deceased (as all the other crew had been killed)
until the Red Cross later advised his parents that
he was a POW.*

burial. The first fire crew fought the fire for two hours before the salvage crew were ready to move in. Immediately the local residents formed a human blockade to prevent the Germans from moving onto the crash site. A standoff ensued for many tense minutes.

The German commanding officer ordered weapons to be readied and issued instructions for the locals to depart otherwise they would be shot. Reluctantly they were forced to retreat, but one man still refused and was taken into custody, later to spend the rest of the war in a prison camp for his defiance.

The Germans knew the plane downed was a Stirling and their salvage crew had collected a total of 7 'dog tags' from the remains of the young Allied airmen. It was well known that a Stirling's usual compliment was seven, so once the tags were found it was naturally assumed that all of the crew had been accounted for.

One of the first people at the crash site had been a local man, Willy Schmidt, with a couple of colleagues. Realising that the Germans would arrive quickly he conducted a simple search for bodies, braving the severe flames and continuing explosions of the mines. Willy heard a cry and went over to the place it came from, some distance from the main wreckage. There in a ditch he spotted a crew member, miraculously thrown just beyond the centre of the inferno, but still badly burned. As he approached, the burned body opened its mouth

Top: Don Jeffs and Bo Sommerby at the Hindsgavl manor house where Don was taken by the Danish Resistance after the crash of MacRobert's Reply. This was in 2003 and was the first time Don had seen it since the crash. Bottom: This was the actual barn where the Resistance hid Don from the German Army shortly after the crash.

to try and speak. Sgt Jeffs was blind, scarred with many burns, and with multiple injuries, but he was alive.

Willy and his friends took the badly injured Don Jeffs down from the crash site to the edge of the forest, by way of a drainage ditch which runs towards what is now a popular tourist beach at Gals Klint. From there he was taken to the nearby Adler estate (now the Hindsgavl Hotel) where Danish Resistance members were summoned to help. To avoid capture by the Germans, Don was kept in the loft of a large shed adjoining the Adler. Incredibly, it still stands to this day.

After several days it became clear that his wounds were not healing and he needed medical assistance. With the help of a local doctor acting as an intermediary, Sven Ulrich, he was handed over to the German army. The German field medical team patched him up in the small hospital in the nearby town of Middelfart, and then he was transported to Rensberg military hospital. It was clear he needed treatment for burns so he was transferred to a specialist unit at Flensberg hospital where he spent a few weeks recovering. Don Jeffs recalls that he received good treatment at Flensburg and remains grateful for their dedication. Once he was considered well enough to travel he was taken from Flensberg to Dulag Luft, the main transit camp for new POWs, and thence to Stalag Luft VIIIB prisoner of war camp in Silesia.

The fate of the bodies of those who died is told in this piece taken by Don Jeffs's son from the book, "Træk fra Odense under den tyske Besættelse" written by Søren Hansen in

1945. It is the only first-hand account he is aware of, and portrays the scene of the funeral of the young men "who had laid down their lives in defence of the right to freedom of another country. A true sacrifice, and never forgotten (on either side of the North Sea)."

It was kindly submitted and translated, by Carsten Høj Rasmussen, a friend of the MacRobert's Reply site from Denmark. It omits Sergeant Maycock from the obituary as he was only later discovered to be part of the crew when Sergeant Jeffs later told the authorities of Maycock's presence on that fateful flight.

The following seven English flyers:

Sergeant Sharp

Sergeant Butterworth

Sergeant Nicholson

Sergeant Spriggs

Pilot (Officer) Hall (Officer) Booth

and Officer Ryan

were buried the 21st May at 7 o'clock from the chapel.

The fliers on the night of May 18th crashed with their aeroplane by the Little Belt nearby Little Belt Bridge. The coffins arrived to Odense on the day of the funeral at about half past five and were received by a German guard of honour.

The coffins were carried into the chapel, and remained there wrapped up in the English flag and under German guard of honour. At seven o'clock the coffins were carried out by German soldiers, while it was preluded from the organ.

At the place in front of the main entrance of the chapel, the coffins were received by the German guard of honour. While the guard of honour presented arms and saluted, the killed were remembered. After that the funeral procession, with the guard of honour in front, moved to the big common grave.

In the first row two double graves were dug, and in the back row one grave was dug for three of those killed. After the coffins were placed above the graves, a German army chaplain pronounced the blessing and made an oration in which he reminisced about the great Olympic Games, the peaceful competitions in which the different countries had participated. The army chaplain pointed out that this peaceful competition was now succeeded by the war. But as long as the war is fought in a way where we bury our enemies, the war is something different from vendetta. The army chaplain mentioned that those killed had fought bravely for their country, and perhaps they had mothers who lament their sons. He expressed the hope that the day will come when German soldiers meet the dead in a foreign country, there also will be mothers who lament these.

After the oration the army chaplain said the Lord's Prayer and officiated at the graveside ceremony. The present German Officers threw earth on the coffins. After this the coffins were slowly lowered into the graves to the tones of a bugle. With full military honours the German guard of honour saluted above the graves and the procession left the cemetery. During the officiation at the graveside ceremony, the bells of the chapel was ringing.

Present at the funeral from Denmark were Captain Buch, Senior Lieutenant E. W. Jørgensen, and Superintendent Frost. On the graves were laid wreaths from Odense Counsil, the Chief Constable in Odense, the 6th Regiment, Consul Muus, the staff of the churchyard and the German army. During the celebration the churchyard was closed off by the Danish police.

Philip Jeffs continues: "Several days after the crash, and when the Germans had left the site, the local residents returned to honour the airmen who had given their lives for

The original ceremony in 1949 that includes relatives of the crew members

the liberation of the occupied countries of Europe. Seeing the huge rock gauged out of the ground by the crashed aircraft, they banded together to roll the massive granite stone back to the place it had originated from, on the edge of the crater formed during the crash within the Gals Klint forest before the Germans had moved it aside. Simple flowers and foliage were laid on the stone as a memorial. It stands in that same spot to this day, still standing guardian over the crater, and is the focus of a memorial service in May every year.

There would be a gap of some four months until the Air Ministry informed Lady MacRobert of the crash in a letter of September 9th 1942:

My dear Lady MacRobert,

The Secretary of State has asked me to write to you and break the sad news of the loss of "MacRobert's Reply," which failed to return from a recent mine-laying sortie.

This magnificent aircraft has had a long and successful career, taking part in many attacks on targets in widely distant parts of Germany and the occupied territories. Its presence in its squadron has been a source of the great spirit of its donor. We are proposing to publish the fact that the aircraft is lost, together with a short narrative of its history. I enclose a copy of the story that has been prepared.

Yours Sincerely
Sir Louis Greig
Personal Air Secretary

The idea of the MacRobert's Reply having been just one aircraft continued in the 'story' that accompanied the letter:

The Stirling bomber, towards the cost of which Lady MacRobert gave the sum of £25,000, is lost. It did not return from a recent sortie. So ends the career of a Bomber Command aircraft which had defied the German A.A. guns and night fighters over some of the most hotly defended targets in Germany and other parts of Europe. It had attacked as far afield as Stettin on the Baltic and Brest on the Atlantic. It had been over the Skoda works at Pilsen in Czechoslovakia. It had been many times in the Ruhr. It had contributed to the successful attacks on the port of Rostock and the Heinkel aircraft works nearby. It had attacked by day as well as by night.

It was in the daylight that an attack on the Scharnhorst and Gneisenau at Brest took place on 18 December. In this attack MacRobert's Reply, as this bomber was called, was attacked by five enemy fighters but shook them off before going on to bomb its objective. It was in one of the raids on the Matford works at Poissy near Paris. It attacked the German naval base at Trondheim.

Before it was lost it did not escape damage in a number of raids but it was always repaired and quickly in the front line again. As is the custom with our four-engine bombers, the same crew did not always fly in MacRobert's Reply. Flight Lieutenant P.J.S. Boggis D.F.C. was most often its captain, but he was not in command on its last sortie.

"You cannot help feeling a sort of affection for your own particular aircraft," said Flight Lieutenant Boggis. "It is funny but no other plane ever seems quite the same. After I had been piloting MacRobert's Reply for a while I was prepared to swear that it was far and away the best bomber in the Squadron and the ground crews are just the same. They take tremendous pride in their jobs and they all felt as I did that MacRobert's Reply was their own."

It is unclear whether Lady MacRobert was ever told that there had been three MacRobert's Reply Stirlings and not just one. In a sense this was not important since it had been made clear to her at the outset that 'the life of a bomber, due to bad luck or quick enemy action, may be extremely short' and that the crest would simply be transferred to another Stirling.

She replied to Sir Archibald Sinclair on September 12th and at the end of her letter emphasised the valour of the crew:

> "If we MacRobert's name might bear
> And all our Squadron be Replies
> In future there'd be hundreds there
> To strike the Nazi from the skies.
>
> So it shall be, and in the fight,
> However named your craft may be;
> Strike hard for Justice and the Right
> To Freedom, won by Victory."

The letter she received in reply on September 27th shows that both she and the Ministry had moved on to the next project, the gift of four Hurricane aircraft. Correspondence had continued between the Air Ministry and Lady MacRobert on a fairly regular basis.

On August 12th, some three months after the crash, she was sent the script of a conversation between Peter Boggis and Flight Sergeant Wilson, the rear gunner, that would be broadcast at 8pm on the Home Service on August 18th 1942. Once again the theme was of there being one aircraft and one crew; the crash wasn't mentioned. This can hardly be regarded as surprising since the MacRobert's Reply story had been one of morale boosting and, importantly, the broadcast would be listened to in Germany for any propaganda opportunities.

The text of the conversation between Boggis and Wilson tells of the regard the two men had for the particular aircraft and describes a raid where they came under heavy attack from flak. The Stirling, for any drawbacks it may have had, was capable of taking a great deal of flak and still making it back home.

Boggis: You always get attached to your aircraft, and you hate flying anyone else's because it isn't anything like so good. After I'd been piloting the MacRobert's Reply for a time, I was quite sure it was twice as good as any other bomber in the squadron. The ground crew get a feeling of pride in their aircraft, as I know the aircrew does. What do you say, Sergeant?

Wilson: Sure, sir, we all feel that the MacRobert's Reply is our own. It's certainly taken us through every sort of bad weather and storm that an aircraft can be asked to face. The trip to Pilsen, for instance.

Boggis: Yes, that was a pretty good test. It's a flight of about 1,200 miles there and back, across Belgium, France and Germany. We climbed up through the cloud over the channel, and when we got to Belgium we found that there was ten tenths cloud below us – that's cloud so dense that it can't be seen through.

Wilson: But that didn't stop Jerry opening up at us with very heavy and accurate flak. They holed the Stirling in several places, though we didn't know that till later. It was too close to be comfortable and we could feel the aircraft shudder. Anyway, it got so darned uncomfortable that we shouted out, "Get weaving skipper, this is getting too much."

Boggis: And you don't start speaking till things get pretty hot. So I didn't waste any time getting cracking. Well, all the way over Europe there was this sea of cloud. We had to rely on astro navigation to get us there, and I think we must have made it, because of all the flak.

Anyway my navigator was always first class at astro navigation. But there wasn't a gap in the clouds so we had to go for an alternative target at Frankfurt. We had to fly above the cloud all the way back, because cumulus cloud is dangerous. It's damp and cold and that means that ice will form on the aircraft if it flies through it. Above the cloud it was minus 26 degrees centigrade, which is cold. But we stuck it, and MacRobert's Reply stuck it.

Wilson: Where we were, there was a bright moon and I had to keep a close look out for night fighters. But they must have been grounded because of the weather for we didn't see any.

Boggis: A good thing, because if one Had appeared we should just have to dive into the cloud and risk icing up. and that's what the Stirling did near Frankfurt, where we ran into a great mountain of cloud. Altogether it was a great relief to find our target, bomb it and set course for home.

Our troubles that night weren't exactly ended. When we got over the Belgian coast again we decided to come down through the cloud. Passing through it we were tossed about by the storm you always find in cumulus cloud, and there were uprushes of air knocking the Stirling about like a boat in the Bay of Biscay. So much so that George, our automatic pilot, couldn't carry on any more and we had to do our own work.

Wilson: Do you remember, Sir, practically the whole crew had to take a hand?

Boggis: Yes…You see, in a Stirling the usual way of coming down is to throttle back the engine so as to go slower. When we did we found that the engines were getting too cold and might fail at any moment, so we had to open up the throttle and lower the undercarriage to reduce speed. Even then the second pilot was kept busy priming the engines one by one to stop them getting too cold, and wiping off the ice as it formed over the instrument dials. In spite of all our care one of the engines on the port side did fail, and we were left with only three engines to keep going on. Then, before we were through the clouds, an engine on the starboard side began to fail and the second pilot had to give all his attention to that.

Wilson: I know I was beginning to wonder if ever we would get through the cloud when the front gunner said on the intercom that we were just coming clear. The ice on my turret and the rest of the aircraft remained for a while but by the time we made it to the coast of England it had all gone and the skipper guided us in quite happy on three engines. Next day we found out that we'd used up most of our petrol and that the aircraft was full of holes from the German flak. But the ground staff soon had her OK and ready for the air again.

The interview ended with a description of the raid on Brest as a result of which Peter Boggis was awarded a D.F.C.

The principal subject of the ongoing correspondence was the proposal that Lady MacRobert would buy four Hurricanes to continue the 'Reply'. She gave a cheque for £20,000. The aircraft were 'in stock' in the Middle East and were named on being allocated to 94 Squadron, Sir Roderick MacRobert's old Squadron. The aircraft were named 'The Lady', 'Sir Roderick', 'Sir Iain' and 'Sir Alasdair' and were flown by New Zealander Flight Lieutenant R. John Pitt Barber, Pilot Officer Arnold Walker, Flight Sergeant Douglas Lawley Stevens Wood, and Sergeant Norman Alderdice, respectively.

Alderdice came from Northern Ireland and had been studying at Queen's University. Wood was from Wolverhampton and had been cost accountant with a 'famous aircraft manufacturer'. Walker was married to a Land Girl and had worked his way up from being a bricklayer to being managing director of his own building company, and Barber had come to England in 1938 and had been a flying instructor before his posting to 94 Squadron. The ground crew mentioned are described as having also serviced Sir Roderick's aircraft.

Lady MacRobert sent a message to these pilots that was read out at a ceremony attended by Air Vice-Marshall McClaughry: "The name MacRobert returns to the squadron on these aircraft. My boys, whose names they bear, were fighters. Their spirit lives on. They inspire confidence and would never let you down. I am proud of them. I shall be proud of you who pilot the MacRobert fighters. My heart and thoughts will be with you. I am confident you will strike hard for victory. I salute everyone in the squadron. May yours be the spirit of the few. God bless you and keep you all. Rachel MacRobert."

There was a third major donation under discussion even whilst the Hurricanes were being handed over and this concerned The House of Cromar, the house built by Lord Aberdeen before Mac bought the estate from him. Rachel MacRobert had in mind the use of the house, which was to be renamed Alastrean House, as a place where RAF personnel could find a place to rest and recuperate. To this day it performs that function. It seems that her action had been precipitated by the possibility that the house would be commandeered by the army!

28 Philip Jeffs
29 Philip Jeffs
30 Don Jeffs

4

CAPTIVITY

In the late summer of 1942, Don Jeffs found himself in Stalag Luft VIIIB at Lamsdorf, Silesia (now southern Poland) which was later renamed Stalag 344. He had first been taken to Dulag Luft near Frankfurt (Oberursel) from the hospital in Rendsburg in Denmark by a German army officer who was travelling back to the eastern front by train. At Dulag Luft he had been interrogated and registered into the prison system. He had then gone briefly to Stalag Luft III, the camp where the Great Escape took place, before ending up at Stalag Luft VIIIB.

Don recalled specific events of his incarceration but as he said with a smile, 'I was too busy staying alive to worry about writing it down'. A number of his fellow prisoners did keep diaries or record their recollections when the memory was still fresh. Many of these are held in the archive of the Imperial War Museum, and it is from these that I attempt to paint a picture of those lost years. Christopher Bowers was a wireless operator with 7 Squadron; James Babcock was a navigator with 150 Squadron; EC Herwin was with 35 Squadron and Sergeant LH Harcus with 115 Squadron.

Flight crew were prepared for what they would experience at Dulag Luft. A number, who later recorded their experiences, expressed a certain amount of respect for the ingenuity of their German interrogators. Many of the crews of aircraft that had crash landed were taken there whilst still in shock from their experience. In Dulag Luft they found friendly British NCO's who would be sympathetic to their predicament. These NCOs were those who had for their own reasons turned collaborator. Their job was to encourage careless talk. All the cells and barrack accommodation were bugged so that even conversations between prisoners would be listened to. Flight crews had prepared for this and the overwhelming majority kept strictly to 'name, rank and number'.

The length of time spent at Dulag Luft varied but was typically one week. Days would be spent in cells for one-to-one questioning by Luftwaffe officers. The PoW would be offered beer and cigarettes and the conversation would be light hearted. This was followed by some hours spent alone as the temperature of the cell rose until it was necessary to strip; even then bodies dripped with sweat. The first congenial interrogations would be followed by more beer and cigarettes. One technique employed to extract information was for the PoW to be given Red Cross forms to complete. Refusal was met by a threat of no Red Cross parcels and no letters from home. Further spells of heat and sweat would follow. It was clear that the interrogators had good sources of intelligence since a further technique was for them to drop details of squadrons and individual and to observe the response. Flight Ops boards would be brought with details of crews, aircraft and missions for PoWs to affirm or deny. The detail was, and was designed to be, unnerving.

Life in Stalag Luft III, which Don experienced for a short time, has been recorded in a book entitled *Wirebound World*, of which a few copies still exist. The one I studied was that belonging to Ernest Abbott who was there from October 1941. Ernest was one of many for whom the camp was a constant nightmare for the remainder of their lives. Prisoners, like Ernest and Don, would enter the 'wirebound world' of the camp and would receive a warm welcome from the inmates already there. In 1942 they were probably sleeping twelve to a hut on three tiered bunks. In this tiny space they would eat hopelessly inadequate rations, sleep in cold and discomfort and pass the long hours of the day. The camp was host to a number of actors including Rupert Davies (who was the first TV Maigret). Just as Don was leaving, there was a move to a new compound where the Germans acceded to a request for a hut that could be made into a theatre. With great ingenuity this was equipped with stage, seating and lighting and many productions of a professional quality were performed. Stalag Luft III at Sagan was the place many of those thousands in Stalag Luft VIIIB dreamed of being sent. Nevertheless it was also a place whose inmates would suffer both physically and mentally from their incarceration for the rest of their lives.

Deep in southern Silesia, Stalag Luft VIIIB was principally a camp for Army PoWs and housed many of those captured at Dunkirk. In a camp within a camp there was the compound reserved for RAF NCOs. These men were not allowed to work and so were never sent on working parties like their army opposite numbers. This had two disadvantages. Firstly, escape was made more difficult; essentially RAF personnel

The Stalag POW camp where Sgt Donald Jeffs was to spend two and a half years before embarking with thousands of other POWs on the Long March to southern Germany in early 1945 ahead of the advancing Russian Army

seeking to escape had first to swap identities with army opposite numbers. Secondly, it meant that life in the camp was a void that only the prisoner himself could fill. Some did, and with great ingenuity. For others this was much more difficult.

James Badcock's account[31] of camp life, taking the huge 10,000 man camp as a whole, spoke of great sport events. There was a high class of football with players including Reg Allen (Queens Park Rangers and Manchester United), Joe Robinson (Blackpool), Harold Roberts (Birmingham), Geordie Harvey (Gateshead) and Tommy Kingsnorth (Northfleet) – gates rarely fell below 8,000. There were English, Australian, New Zealanders and South Africans and so both rugby and cricket were played between the national representatives. The South African cricket team was led by former test wicket keeper Billy Wade.

A good deal of football was played between barracks. The huts, or barracks, in Stalag Luft VIIIB were brick built with concrete floors standing in pairs in the separate compounds. Men slept on three tier bunks, some 120 to a barracks. All food was taken in the barracks and washing facilities were shared between the neighbouring buildings. The playing of football, but also boxing and other sports, ensured a healthy rivalry.

It wasn't just sport. In time, teachers among the PoWs saw the value in setting up a school in order to keep the men occupied. Books were supplied through the Red Cross by the Bodleian Library in Oxford and even exam papers were posted from England for the PoWs to sit. James Badcock sat his Institute of Secretaries exams; Christopher Bowers his City and Guilds Carpentry. There were many more and a whole range of subjects were offered.

In the RAF compound, in the absence of work and the activities enjoyed in the outer compound between non-RAF POW's, long hours were spent playing bridge and chess and gambling for cigarettes. Christopher Bowers, recalling his experience, swore never again to handle a playing card, and he never did.

Theatre also featured in the life of Stalag Luft VIIIB and one of the inmates was Denholm Elliott who would later play the hapless RAF weather forecaster in the film 'A Bridge Too Far', amongst many other roles. Elliott spoke of his time as a PoW,[32] and this is his description of his arrival:

"It was a clear night with a full moon and we went through the prison gates and found ourselves on very sandy soil with fir trees silhouetted on the little hills all around the camp, which was quite a big place. They took away my fur-lined boots and my fleece-lined flying jacket. The reason why I originally wanted to join the air crew was because I really liked the look of that warm bomber jacket. Anyway they gave me a pair of really repellent clogs and an awful army great coat, and instantly one looked like a prisoner.

"We were silently clomping up this long sandy road with barbed wire on either side and compounds, Indians in one and the Air Force in another and the Palestinians in another and this sort of thing. We came to one guarded barbed wire gate and in we went. We were directed towards a hut, a long, low hut and we went in. It was hundreds of feet long, pitch black, total darkness, three of us. A voice said, 'Find yourselves somewhere to sleep the night and I will talk to you in the morning.' We stumbled over all sorts of things. We didn't know where we were. The bunks were three tier with the top bunk two-and-a-half feet from the ceiling and the bottom tier virtually on the floor. Mattresses were a sort of sacking filled with straw.

Another PoW had been in the camp during the exceptionally cold winter of 1940/41 and recalled ice on the inside of the windows some three inches thick from the condensation of the breath of so many men in such a small space. Windows there may have been, but not much glass. In time the missing pains were patched with the sides of Red Cross parcels.

EC Herwin recalled the difficulty of sleep. He starts though with lavatories:

"I'll commence on a delicate subject. Lavatories – they are foul! Picture a deep pit with a brick wall around it and a leaky roof. Windows without panes and pardon the reference – seating accommodation for forty – privacy impossible. Imagine one's discomfort in winter with temperature 30 degrees below.

"Talking about winter, another in this place almost brings suicidal tendencies. God the last was hell! Hands chained, very little food and even less warmth in the barracks. Feet were constantly freezing on the stone floor. Unable to lie on beds and waiting in relays to sit down on insufficient forms. Even at night one could not forget the place in the unconsciousness of sleep. Two blankets cannot keep out intense cold and even though all available clothing is piled on, one remains awake shivering and trying to find a little comfort in a cigarette."

This same writer referred also to the dreadful fleas that got everywhere. The reference to chains brings one of Don's most enduring memories. He recalled no particular ill- treatment except that following the Dieppe raid in August 1942. He recalled that all RAF prisoners were handcuffed for ten months in response to the treatment of German prisoners by the Canadians who took part in the Dieppe raid and who bound their captives hand and foot.

James Badcock recalled that the handcuffs and chains came some six weeks after the first repercussion from the raid: "In September 1942 conditions in Stalag VIIB were extremely tough – food was scarce and the Germans were really pushing us around. The survivors of the Dieppe Raid (Aug 19th 1942) were brought in and then it happened. Tough NCOs arrived. Hands tied from 8 until noon and from 13 to 21, including using latrines. Bound with twine taken from Red Cross parcels. Nothing to do except play cards and talk. Chafing wrists and setting up running sores which would cross infect. After six weeks, hand cuffs with chains came. In November the guards departed for the eastern front and were replaced by second-class soldiers who had less control.

Don Jeffs also recalled a more aggressive attitude by his captors as the RAF began the more general bombing of cities in the latter part of the war. Food was scarce. The accounts vary in detail on just how scarce. To James Badcock a typical days food was as follows:

7.30 half pint of mint

11.30 potato ration 4 per man

12.00 noon 1 pint of swede soup

14.00 bread ration 6 men to one loaf

15.00 pat of ersatz margarine or jam

15.30 half pint of mint

Denholm Elliott, though, wrote of looking forward to the evening's food, hoping that it would be enough not to keep him awake with hunger. When asked what they did all day, Don Jeffs response was brief and to the point: "We played Bridge." Don also made radios. He told me with a sparkle in his eye that near to the camp there was a tank depot where seemingly unlimited lengths of wire could be 'borrowed'. His expertise learnt in the Scouts and from Marconi enable him to make many crystal sets and so enabled many in the RAF camp to listen to the news of the progress of the war.

Radios were also a feature of Stalag Luft III and I suspect all camps. In *Wirebound World*, HP Clark writes of crystal sets: designed and built in the camp with every component made by hand with available materials. Variable condensers were made from old biscuit tins, cut to shape, and insulated by melting down gramophone records. Paper formers held coils wound to match condensers, while a piece of paper with a pencil line acted as a resistor. The valve was the only component of a complete receiving and transmitting station that wasn't manufactured in the camp without tools or special appliances.

As with all PoWs, letters could be written home and letters from home would arrive intermittently. Don Jeffs was keen that his parents should write to the parents of the eight who had died in the crash, and a regular correspondence developed between them.

Don remained in the camp until January 1945 when he and the other prisoners in the camp left to march westward as the Germans retreated from the advancing Russian army. Don told of the extreme cold and how many PoWs died. There was little food, warm clothing or ways of keeping clean. As they covered the 700 mile journey they saw the bodies of US airmen hanging from lampposts in retaliation for the bombing of German cities. He recalls that the local population were not friendly and the German guards were present as much to protect their prisoners as to prevent escape. Escape in any event would not have been possible given their appalling physical condition. Don observed that those who survived tended to be those men who had come from a background where they had had to struggle. It demanded a tremendous toughness of mind and body. Another memory was having to make a five mile detour around Dresden and how, even at that distance, the stench was appalling.

This short paragraph clouds what was amongst the most horrific episodes of this dreadful war. I am indebted to those survivors who recorded their accounts of what they endured. Denholm Elliott began his account in a rather grand way, but this didn't last:

"When we marched out of Stalag VIIIB there was heavy snow on the ground and an endless road ahead, rather like Napoleon's retreat from Moscow. Prisoners shuffled along with guards on either side. On and on they went and after some hours people began to jettison their cherished little possessions, scattering them on the snow as they went along. They were too heavy to carry. None of us was strong and the walking seemed endless.

"At the end of the first day we were put into an enormous barn for the night. I had clung onto the rear of a cart drawn by a horse for the last miles because I was very very weak. When we got into the barn, I just threw myself down on the snow and burst into tears."

James Badcock was more matter of fact: "On January 23rd 1945 at Stalag 344, 3,000 odd British PoWs with 2 hours' prior notice began an epic journey aided by bayonets and the rifle butts of the German army. Without proper kit and with little food, and in the intense cold of the Silesian winter, we were forced out – away from the advancing Russians.

"There were three columns of about 1,200 men each accompanied by guards who were in sheer panic. Quo vadimus? Nobody knew. The first couple of days set the pattern. We

hadn't learned the drill yet and felt awful. We were pushed on
and on. When we did rest, we just flopped down in the snow
and then, when we resumed, suffered untold agonies from our
aching limbs which had got set in cold whilst we rested.

"Naturally our casualties in the first days were high, from
torn muscles – muscles we did not know we had – rifle butts
etc. Sleeping accommodation was primitive. We were herded
into small sheds like cattle. It was quite impossible to lie down,
and if you could wash you were fortunate. Attending to the
wants of nature were a work of art."

Diaries kept on *The Long March*, as it was subsequently
called, tell of day after day of marching but also days of rest
when bodies were literally incapable of walking further.

The detail of what was experienced on the march varied
depending upon which column you were in. EC Herwin kept
a diary, which he edited in January 1994. On February 4th
1945, he had this to say of the horrors they endured: "Stalag
VIIIA [VIIIA was some miles to the west of VIIIB] was a
complex of prisons on the outskirts of Gorlitz. On arrival we
were herded into a Russian prison amongst Russians, most
of whom were without legs or arms. We learned that the Russians were political prisoners, and that this was an offshoot
of another concentration camp. The conditions were truly
horrific. We were in a pen size about 50x50 yds. In the pen
were 3 concrete huts each of which accommodated 100 to
120 prisoners.

"The huts were without heating and where there should have been windows and doors, there were gaping holes. The huts were surrounded by a sea of mud. The hut floors were thick with mud. The layout was somewhat similar to a 1950s battery hen house. One slept on a rack or open shelf and as stated before, the slats were entirely covered in a thick layer of the previous occupier's bloody faeces.

"The bottom racks were, if possible, in even worse condition because of the mud brought in on the feet of occupants. The pen was enclosed by barbed wire fences between which were the customary coils of barbed wire. There was no laid on water for drinking or washing. We were left to rot in this place. No one with any authority would come to relieve our distress. We were so overcrowded that lying fully clothed on the racks one could not turn over at night. The toilet consisted of a pit full of liquid faeces surrounded by a quagmire over with was an excrement-covered hole upon which we were supposed to sit. We were filled with despair."

Just seven days later, the same writer recorded that the column was approaching Dresden. "Finished the day's march at Bautzen and spent the night in the gymnasium of a very large barracks. We were given hot soup. The first hot food for over three weeks. If only we weren't starved and had dry clothing, this march would be an interesting experience."

The columns seem to have progressed at slightly different paces. As already mentioned, Don Jeffs recalled the stench of Dresden after the bombing. James Babcock recorded,

"I went outside [the church where they were spending the night] and laid down by a tombstone to watch the raid. I had never seen anything like it. There was one incessant roar as the bombs went down. The target was, I believe, Dresden."

A couple of days later an entry in a diary kept by GA Hemsley gives glimpses of humanity creeping into the marching hell: "The best billet we've had. We were in the school in the centre of the town and the people were bringing soup and bread as fast as they can. Had another rest here. Six of us went down into the town to help get the shop ready for dinner. The women here are very beautiful and much smarter than the Germans. The guards don't like it because everywhere we go the people make us very welcome and wave to us as we march by."

The columns split further and progressed slowly through the frozen wasteland that was Germany. Villages and towns destroyed by bombing; the local people hostile to the prisoners, particularly, Badcock records, to the Palestinians. The guards were replaced by Hitler Youth who made up for their inexperience with their hostility. Food became more and more scarce. Red Cross parcels became a memory. Then at the end of February, dysentery struck.

James Badcock writes: "This would have been bad enough in the best circumstances but on the road, with no medical supplies to combat it, it was deadly. As the victims became worse, they became unrecognisable. During this week we had marched nearly 100kms on 3/8ths of a loaf and a small issue of raw meat.

"During the next three days we pushed on through Hostedt and Mulligan to Urbich. We were constantly stopped for air raids, and on Thursday March 1st two chaps died during the night. What with our increasing weakness and the stoppages we couldn't make the daily journeys nearly so fast and walked late into the late evening: that meant even more trouble over billeting and no food because it was too late. We were lucky if we could get a wash in four days now and it was a miracle we weren't all lousy."

With the March splitting into so many smaller columns there was no single end to it. Prisoners and guards alike became aware of the Allied advance and guards tried to turn the columns round to escape. Prisoners were by then so exhausted that far from turning they just ground to a halt.

James Badcock was first told that his March had ended on February 27th and then again on March 12th where "we linked up with the main column and entered Stalag IXC…on 26 March Jerry tried to force us out again to walk away from the Americans this time. A few went – most of us went sick and were left behind….the death roll mounted and, even after we were relieved by the Americans, on Good Friday [30 March] we lost as many as sixteen. Those of us who did weather the storm were certainly much slimmer than before. Six hundred miles, on practically no food, had reduced me from a sturdy 12 stone 10 lbs to a streamlined 8 stone 6 lbs."

Don Jeffs finished up at Stalag XIIB, a place he describes as 'grim' with no barracks and POWs sleeping wherever a spare piece of ground could be obtained. They had no supplies or bedding, virtually no food, and their German guards were also in a very poor way. However, shortly after their arrival he recalled hearing machinery in the distance getting closer, then the British tanks of the 11th Hussars driving through the barbed wire that had kept them captive. The British Army was so distressed to see the thin and desperate POWs that they threw down chocolate and other 'treats' that they had, but after so long living on scraps and soup made from scavenged potatoes, the well meaning gesture simply resulted in cases

A welcome home street party for Donald Jeffs by the people of Long Eaton, Nottingham after his return from many years as a POW

of vomiting as stomachs could not cope with the rich sugary food. Don Jeffs recalls an overwhelming feeling at that time – for the first time since May 1942, he was a free man again.

5
HOME

Don Jeffs returned to England by Dakota on April 26th 1945. He used his back pay from his promotion to Warrant Officer to open a shop selling first radio and other electrical appliances and then motor bikes.

In 1948 the Danish people expressed a wish for a memorial to be established to mark the site of the crash. Don visited the site and took photographs of the graves. He then wrote to each of the families of those who had died; the ensuing correspondence reveals a glimpse at the human tragedy.

Frank Sharp's mother, writing from her home in Kingston upon Thames, was doubtful whether the remains that had been buried were truly of her son. She later wrote to say that she would like to attend. Sergeant Butterworth's mother, writing from Oldham, was delighted to have received the invitation for the ceremony on May 18th 1949 and "to hear of the kindness of the people in Middlefart. Squadron Leader John Hall's mother, writing from Wymondham in Norfolk, also accepted the invitation and spoke of her visit to Sergeant Spriggs' mother in Bristol and how much she had valued her own correspondence with Don's mother when he had been PoW. Bobbie Nicholson's mother, writing from the Dog & Duck Inn at Walkington Nr Beverley, told how her husband had become ill with worry about his son and how she saw herself as lucky to have had Don to tell her what had happened.

Don received a letter from Denmark reporting on the ceremony and how it had been attended by family members of Hall, Butterworth, Sharp, Spriggs and Nicholson. No reply had ever been received from Neville Booth's parents and Buck Ryan's family were on the other side of the world.

Squadron Leader John Hall's name was added to the War Memorial at Wymondham. Flying Officer Neville Booth's name was included in the War Memorial at Lancing College and the War memorial in Eglwysbach in North Wales where the family had a house.

Thus there remained Sergeant Maycock who had been on the fatal flight just to learn about GEE navigation. In 1999 a group of people from Odense had worked their way through reports and testimonies dating back to May 1942, and the evidence of Don Jeffs, and had collected enough evidence to be able to convince the Commonwealth Graves Commission that Maycock actually had been buried with

Top: A guard of honour by 15 Squadron RAF at the crash site memorial stone in the Gals Klint forest in Denmark. Bottom: A piper plays a solemn lament for the fallen crew

*15 Squadron RAF paying respect to some of their own who paid the
ultimate sacrifice*

his comrades on May 21st 1942[33]. His name was added to the memorial.

The Memorial is tended with great care by the Danish people and each year a ceremony is held on May 5th in memory of those young men who died. This date coincides with the Danish Liberation remembrance. It is the anniversary of the end of the occupation of Denmark by Nazi Germany. The German forces withdrew from Denmark on May 5th 1945 following their surrender to the Allies. The anniversary of this event is now celebrated as Liberation Day and special events are held on the occasion including remembering those Allied airmen who lost their lives in that struggle.

Lady MacRobert continued her support for the war effort and for the RAF by undertaking many speaking arrangements but also by setting up the MacRobert Trusts that continue to benefit RAF people but also engineers to this day.

Peter Boggis took command of XV Squadron in 1947 and eventually retired from the RAF in 1967 having attained the rank of Squadron Leader. He continued to visit Lady Mac-Robert until her death in 1954. He died in 2010 at the age of 91. His obituary in the Scotsman tells how in "March 2003 he returned to the MacRobert Trust principal home, Douneside House on Deeside, to help unveil a magnificent bronze sculpture of the Stirling close to the resting place of Lady MacRobert. It is startling bronze and depicts the MacRobert Reply coming in to land."

Top: The current MacRobert's Reply Tornado operated by 15 Squadron RAF based at Loss-iemouth in Scotland. Bottom: The Buccaneer of 15 squadron that was named MacRobert's Reply. This was after the war and before the more recent Tornado aircraft that now bears the name.

XV Squadron's Association website tells how: "The association with MacRobert's Reply, which had ceased in 1942, was rekindled in April 1982 at Mildenhall, when Squadron Leader Peter Boggis DFC performed an unveiling ceremony. Two Buccaneers and the Hawker Hunter from XV Squadron had flown across from Laarbruch to attend the annual Mildenhall Register reunion at the Squadron's former wartime base. One of the Buccaneers, 'XT287', coded 'F', had been selected to be the first aircraft since 1942 to bear the name MacRobert's Reply and was also adorned with the MacRobert family crest. Although he was unaware of it at the time, when Peter Boggis dedicated the aircraft as 'MacRobert's Reply' he was starting a tradition that has continued to the present day. Since then every XV Squadron aircraft coded 'F' has carried that name and crest.

Jeffs tells of Donald's only other return to Denmark: "My mother had passed away on Christmas Day 2001, and after the funeral we decided to honour a long-standing wish she had maintained to see my father return to Denmark, something he was reluctant to do as it held so many memories.

"We went across for the 60th anniversary remembrance in May 2002 and it was an extremely moving experience as he had only returned once before in 1947. We visited the crash site in Gals Klint Forest and the cemetery in Odense where the crew are buried, both visits prior to the main remembrance services at those locations so he could have some quiet time to reflect and remember

This hugely emotional picture shows Don Jeffs in 2003 on the Little Belt Bridge where the German anti-aircraft battery had been placed which shot down the MacRobert's Reply. His thoughts at this moment must be very painful as he reflects upon the loss of his crewmates.

Top: Don Jeffs at the International Bomber Command Centre. Bottom: Don Jeffs searches for his crewmates on the panels of the International Bomber Command Centre memorial garden in Lincoln during the unveiling ceremony where he was an honoured guest.

his crewmates. At the end of a long day I took a photograph of him standing in reflective mood on the Little Belt Bridge, a photograph that remains a powerful image to this day.

"It is hard to imagine his feelings standing at the spot where the plane was fatally hit by anti-aircraft fire, and a little further west crashed into Gals Klint forest where all of his crewmates were killed. It certainly brought a lump to my throat taking the picture, but I am glad I did as it will always be a powerful reminder of the suffering and sacrifice made by many thousands of young people during the war. I hope we never forget them."

At the unveiling of the Bomber Command memorial in Lincoln in 2015, Don Jeffs, an invited VIP guest, was present to see the current MacRobert's Reply Tornado fly past the memorial in salute.

Phil Jeffs continues, "As the commentator, Dan Snow of the BBC, described the history of the MacRobert's Reply and the fact that the sole survivor was in the invited audience, the crowd stood and applauded. And as my father gave the MacRobert's Reply Tornado a wave, the story seemed complete somehow."

31 James Oliver Badcock, Life in Stalag VIIIB German Prisoner of War Camp and after World War Two (99/47/1

32 Private Papers of D M Elliott CBE IWM Documents.7697

33 Philip Jeffs

*Sgt Donald Jeffs with the scale
replica of MacRobert's Reply
commissioned by Hornby
Triang with design input from
Philip Jeffs*

Without the contributions of the following individuals, this book would not exist. A heartfelt thank you to:

Alex Richardson

Alex Norton

Andy Alexander

Andy Kidd

Angela Hayes

Aksel Sommerby

Bill Read

Bo Sommerby

Carsten Høj Rasmussen

Cheryl Grass

Chris Payne

Clive Elverstone

Di Ablewhite

Darren Sladden

Dave Barsby

Dave Newson

David Kavanagh

David Toube

Dee Boneham

Dereck McCready

Dilys Guthrie

Emily Smith

Frances Jeffs

Gloria Bradley

Henrik Hansen

Jacqueline Scholefield

Janice Allen

Jon Nixon

Jonny Cracknell

Kaj Olesen

Kaj Voigt

Karen Brough

Karen Cox

Karl Miller

Kirsten-Jane Andersen

Laura Biddiscombe

Lesley Jeffs

Lesley McLeod

Lisbeth Behrendt

Martin Alford

Martin Jeffs

Martin Lynn

Martin Tozer

Michael Sparkes

Michael Hagger

Mike Jeffs

Morten Eriksen
Paul Froome
Peter Sinclair
Rebecca Jeffs
Reg Woodward
Robert Lawson
Robert Davies
Roger Leivers
Ryan Main
Scott Jeffs
Steve George
Sue Bridgwater
Tara Farman
Thomas Blackwood
Tim Barratt
Tracey Jeffs
Vanessa Steadman

Printed in Great Britain
by Amazon